Sagacious Life Quotes

An assortment of intuitive thoughts compiled to
create amazing passages to nourish the soul

13TH & JOAN

For permission requests, write to the publisher, addressed "Attention: Permissions Coordinator," 205 N. Michigan Avenue, Suite #810, Chicago, IL 60601. 13th & Joan books may be purchased for educational, business or sales promotional use. For information, please email the Sales Department at sales@13thandjoan.com.

Printed in the U. S. A.

First Printing, July 2023.

Library of Congress Cataloging-in-Publication Data has been applied for.

ISBN: 978-1-953156-66-2

A DEDICATION TO MY MOTHER

Growing up with both parents and a large family, my mother provided strong spiritual guidance to everyone in her path by sharing biblical and inspirational quotes. These quotes were so profound that her guidance still lives within me today, and eventually inspired me to share some of my own quotes with all of you. I hope that my words will help someone along their journey and encourage someone to be the best version of themselves just like my mother's words did for me.

Mother, this book is dedicated to you, a strong, spiritual Black woman with a heart of gold and a smile that was bright like the sun. A woman who was always extending her hand to aid somebody in need. A true humanitarian by any means necessary. A rare breed indeed.

Proverbs 31:25-26 "She is clothed in strength and dignity and she laughs without fear of the future. When she speaks, her words are wise, and she gives instructions with kindness."

I love you and I am so grateful for the wisdom, confidence, and encouragement along with the inherited gift of discernment to see life through clearer lenses than many others at an early age. To be able to stand and speak before the church congregation with memorized speeches that were three to four times longer than the other children's. Yes I complained, because at the time, I could not see your vision nor the foundation you were creatively preparing for me to stand on later in life. Even though you are no longer here, I still hear your voice saying, "Baby girl, you can do this." And yes, Mother, I can, with your prayers and Psalm 91 embedded deeply in my heart. Thank you for making me the extraordinary woman I am today.

I can hear you singing the words to this song, Mother:

"If I can help somebody
as I pass along, If I can
cheer somebody with
a word or a song,
If I can show somebody
their traveling wrong,
Then my living will
not be in vain."

Song lyrics by: "Alma Irene Androzzo"
Performed by: Mahalia Jackson

EPIGRAPH

Blessed is the man that walketh not in the counsel of the ungodly, nor standeth in the way of sinners, nor sitteth in the seat of the scornful. But his delight is in the law of the Lord; and in his law doth he meditate day and night.

(Psalm 1: 1-2)

PREFACE

I spent many years of my life, starting from a teenager, trying to understand the reason people are the way they are. Inevitably, I realized it is what it is and we have to identify and grasp the ways we can help ourselves first, by every means necessary, and I often choose to use words of wisdom.

ACKNOWLEDGEMENTS

"I have learned that people will forget what you said, people will forget what you did, but they will never forget how you made them feel."
Maya Angelou.

I am grateful to everyone I have encountered in my life that has contributed to me being the woman I am today. Sometimes it takes a village, and believe me, as a youth, I was definitely guided and encouraged by a few amazing people in my neighborhood where I grew up, school and church. But it all started with my parents. Knowing their first jobs were in a Georgia field picking cotton at age four made me want to work that much harder to achieve my personal goals. None of it was easy, but I know for sure that I have put forth great effort to make sure you both were proud of your baby girl and all that I have accomplished thus far .

To Ronald, Terrica, Brian, Malachi, Imani, Lorenzo and Chwalbwa, my sister in heaven, thank you all for loving me and understanding this new journey in my life.

Lastly, my dear Ardre and the 13th & Joan staff, thank you. Thank you for the motivation to pick up a pen and paper. God bless you.

INSPIRATIONAL QUOTES

Enjoy your life.
There is someone
hoping and praying
to be a part of it.

Let go of things that clutter
your mind and spirit.
Seek only what brings
your soul peace.

Being knowledgeable
makes you powerful.

You are valuable,
which is why the weak
ones keep trying to
lower your price tag
with hurtful descriptions
of your character.

Extraordinary describes
the new and better you
who has healed from
past life mistakes.

Sometimes without warning,
God will test us so that
we can truly see how
important our work is
to others.

14

No one ever said that
what you want in life is
simple, but it will require
you to be consistent.

Only keep company with those that elevate you emotionally, mentally, and spiritually.

Stay near to people
that keep you laughing
and smiling even after
they walk away.

Don't forget you matter more.
Stop being concerned
about what hurt people
say about you.

When love is in the heart,
no place on this green
earth is too far.

Always be choosey in
your life choices.

Happy moments will appear when you let go of spending time with sadness.

Keep close to those
that bring light into
your dark room.

Change things up this time, take a completely different path and have faith in yourself.

It's your job to share that
knowledge which has
brought you great prosperity.

44

Be capable of being the hero you seek in others.

True friends should compliment who you are as a person.

38

Make sure their vibe
is your vibe;
don't settle for
anything less.

Compromise only if it doesn't cause you pain, and it comes directly from your heart.

41

Strive to win, and even if you lose, it still feels like a win because you put forth great effort to get that far.

SELF LOVE QUOTES

Just be you.
What others think
does not matter.

Never be afraid to be the amazing you the world has been waiting to see.

Always choose your
happiness first.

It's never too late to pursue the dream that makes your heart smile.

Reveal the Queen
within you and
never forget how beautiful,
intelligent, and important
you are to you.

If it's not helping you grow,
let it go.

One of the most valuable
things to know in
life is yourself.

You are the keeper of your happiness, and being difficult sometimes is often necessary.

Do the unthinkable;
love yourself even when you
think you are undeserving.

64

Challenge yourself to the maximum and see just how powerful you really are.

Life is simple when
you're being yourself.

The biggest commitment
you must make in life must
be to your own happiness.

My confidence bothers
you because I am all
that you wish to be.

Loving yourself is
not selfish,
it's required.

LIFE
QUOTES

Always show people the best version of you because second chances are not always guaranteed.

You can use a lot of kind words, but only your actions validate your truth.

We all have flaws, but don't let it dictate your journey nor limit how high you place your goals.

Remember that you
have tomorrow,
Don't stress about what
does not happen today.

Forgiveness does not erase
everything completely,
it simply gradually fades
the visible pain you
wear on the outside.

Check your own spirit
when desires within
you encourage the
mistreatment of others.

Jealousy always displays
itself when happy
moments are present.

Never expect loyalty from anyone that does not respect your boundaries.

When dishonesty sacrifices
another persons character,
karma is never far away.

Betrayal by someone whom you trusted hurts the deepest, but remember that you will heal.

A quick recipe for failure
in your life is to not
accept wisdom that
influences growth.

97

Your opinions matter to you,
but not always to others.

May all the mistakes
you made yesterday
remain behind you.

You already know it's wrong, stop wasting space in your head thinking of ways to make it seem right.

No matter what comes
from their mouth,
pay attention to
their actions.

It's hard for them to
look in your eyes
when they have no good
intentions for you later.

They're not smiling like you because they were hoping you would fail.

Trust and respect are required if you want to build a good relationship with anyone.

Never let the flowers in your head mask the real truth about someone who clearly does not respect you.

114

Always be sure the task is worth your valuable time because nothing in life is free.

Waste no time on people
that don't add value
to your greatness.

If a friend don't elevate your name in a conversation that you're absent from, keep it moving without them in your life.

Being curious is a sign of brilliance hard at work.

Real love will always
find its way back.

Smiling can be very confusing to a person that seeks to witness your failure.

Everybody is not friend material.
Listen closely with open eyes while their truth is revealed.

No matter what you say,
the face always gets a
delayed reaction when
dishonest feelings
are present.

Sometimes your dreams of success makes it possible to see your achievements prematurely in order to get you moving forward in your endeavors.

The silence from those close to you during the celebration of your big accomplishments exposes their true feelings.

144

Second chances are
not guaranteed.
Get it right as if it was
your last opportunity.

Watch the ones you trust while in the midst of a crisis in your life.

Trust has no value inside of
a heart filled with jealousy.

Progress is progress.

Your placement in life was done deliberately and designed according to the purpose our God has created just for you

NOTES

NOTES

NOTES

NOTES

NOTES

About the Author: Cassie Maura Rahming
Photography By KeyFootage

ABOUT THE AUTHOR: CASSIE MAURA RAHMING

Cassie Maura Rahming is an African American woman from Miami, Florida with a strong passion for the arts and helping others. She has a bachelor's degree in Public Administration, and is a former Enforcement Officer. Cassie is a youth mentor and a proud member of Zeta Phi Beta Sorority, Incorporated. She also serves as the co-founder of No Dancer Left Behind, Incorporated, a non-profit organization created to mentor, educate, and expose less fortunate youth, ages 6 to 18, to the art of dance. Their mission is to use various genres of dance to bridge cultures by awarding free scholarships to selected youth to participate with the program in Lauderhill, Florida.